Penguin English

Introducing Language and Society

Peter Trudgill taught in the Department of Linguistic Science at the University of Reading from 1970 to 1986, and is currently Professor of Sociolinguistics at the University of Essex. He has carried out linguistic field-work in Britain, Greece and Norway, and has lectured in most European countries, Canada, the United States, Australia, New Zealand, India, Thailand, Hong Kong, Malawi and Japan. Peter Trudgill is the author of *Sociolinguistics: an Introduction to Language and Society*; *Accent, Dialect and the School*; *English Accents and Dialects*; *International English*; *Applied Sociolinguistics*; *Dialects in Contact*; *On Dialect*; *Language in the British Isles*; *Dialectology*; *Bad Language* with Lars Andersson; and other books and articles on sociolinguistics and dialectology.

Other Titles in the Series

Introducing English Grammar

Introducing Language and Mind

Introducing Linguistics

Introducing Phonetics

Introducing LANGUAGE AND SOCIETY

Peter Trudgill

PENGUIN ENGLISH

PENGUIN ENGLISH

Published by the Penguin Group
Penguin Books Ltd, 27 Wrights Lane, London W8 5TZ, England
Penguin Books USA Inc., 375 Hudson Street, New York, New York 10014, USA
Penguin Books Australia Ltd, Ringwood, Victoria, Australia
Penguin Books Canada Ltd, 10 Alcorn Avenue, Toronto, Ontario, Canada M4V 3B2
Penguin Books (NZ) Ltd, 182-190 Wairau Road, Auckland 10, New Zealand

Penguin Books Ltd, Registered Offices: Harmondsworth, Middlesex, England

First published 1992
1 3 5 7 9 10 8 6 4 2

Printed in England by Clays Ltd, St Ives plc
Set in 10/13 pt Lasercomp Times Roman

Introduction to the series

The aim of this series is to meet a need which has often been expressed by students encountering linguistics for the first time – to have a brief, clear and convenient guide to central concepts in the various branches of the subject, which would help them develop painlessly a sense of its range and depth. The idea is to provide a comprehensive outline of an area, which can be used as a general backup for lectures, a supplementary index for textbooks, and an opportune aid for revision. The information is organized alphabetically, for convenience of look-up, but it is presented discursively, with copious cross-references. The result is a somewhat unconventional kind of reference book – half-dictionary, half-encyclopedia – but one which offers considerable gains in accessibility and comprehension. The order of headwords is based on word-by-word alphabetization.

We have chosen topics for the first books in the series which are widely taught in introductory undergraduate and postgraduate courses. Along with linguistics itself, we have dealt with phonetics, English grammar, sociolinguistics, and psycholinguistics. Each has been written by an acknowledged leader in the field, in consultation with the general editor, and the result is a series which I believe conveys with authority, clarity, currency and consistency the core elements of this fascinating subject.

David Crystal

Acknowledgements

I am very grateful to the following for their help and advice in the preparation of this volume: Jenny Cheshire, David Crystal, Jean Hannah, James Milroy and Lesley Milroy.

Abstand language (German /ˈapštant/) A **variety** of language which is regarded as a **language** in its own right, rather than a **dialect**, by virtue of being very different in its linguistic characteristics from all other languages. Such is the degree of linguistic **distance** (German **Abstand**) between this variety and other languages that, unlike **Ausbau languages**, there can be no dispute as to its language status. Basque, the language spoken in northern Spain and southwestern France, is a good example of an Abstand language. It is clearly a single language, because its dialects are similar. And it is clearly a language rather than a dialect because, since it is not related historically to any other European languages, it is completely different in its grammar, vocabulary and pronunciation from the neighbouring languages, French and Spanish.

accent The way in which people pronounce when they speak. Since everybody pronounces when they speak – everyone has phonetics and phonology – everybody speaks with an accent. A speaker's accent may relate to where they are from geographically (e.g., a London accent, an American accent). It may relate to their social background (e.g., an upper-class accent, or, in England, an **RP** accent). Or it may relate to whether they are a native speaker or not (e.g., a French accent, a foreign accent). Accent and **dialect** normally go together (Yorkshire dialect is spoken with a Yorkshire accent) but British sociolinguists distinguish between the two because the RP accent and the **Standard English** dialect are not always combined.

accommodation The process whereby participants in a conversation adjust their **accent**, **dialect** or other language characteristics according to the language of the other participant(s). Accommodation theory, as developed by the British social psychologist of language, Howard Giles, stresses that accommodation can take one of two major forms: **convergence**, when speakers modify their accent or dialect, etc., to make them resemble more closely those of the people they are speaking to; and, less usually, **divergence**, when, in order to signal social distance or disapproval, speakers make their language more unlike that of their interlocutors. Accommodation normally takes place during **face-to-face interaction**.

acrolect A **variety** or **lect** which is socially the highest, most prestigious variety in a social **dialect continuum**. Other varieties lower down the social dialect continuum in terms of social status are known as **mesolects** and **basilects**. This terminology is particularly common in the discussion of the sociolinguistic situation in **post-creole continuum** communities such as Jamaica, where **Standard English** is the acrolect, Jamaican **Creole** the basilect, and linguistically intermediate varieties the mesolects.

acts of identity According to the British sociolinguist Robert LePage, any **speech act** performed by an individual. In any given situation, speakers will select from the range of **varieties** available to them in their **verbal repertoires** depending on which personal and social identity they wish to project. By selecting a pronunciation or grammatical form or word associated with and symbolic of a particular group in society, they will be projecting their identity as a member of that social group rather than some other identity. **Accommodation** of both the convergence and divergence type can be interpreted as constituting an act of identity.

actuation problem One of a number of problems pointed to by the American sociolinguist William Labov in connection with the study of linguistic change within the field of **secular linguistics**. The actuation problem is the problem for the linguist of explaining why a particular linguistic change is set in motion in the first place. Historical linguists may be quite good at accounting for particular sound changes or grammatical changes, but why do changes start where and when they do, and not at some other place or time? A related problem, as discussed by Labov, is the **embedding problem**.

address forms Words and phrases used to address other people in conversations, meetings, letters, etc. Address forms may include pronouns such as *you*, titles such as *Sir* and *Madam*, names such as *John* and *Mr Smith*, and endearments and expressions such as *mate*, *buddy*, *dear*, *honey*. In all communities, there are norms concerning who uses which form to whom, what the social implications are of using one form or another, and on which occasions particular forms may be used. In Britain, it would be unusual to address a friend by title plus surname, e.g., *Mr Smith*, and more usual to address them by their first name, e.g., *John*. In many languages, speakers also have to select second-person pronouns, corresponding to English *you*, according to sociolinguistically appropriate norms. Selection usually involves a choice of **T and V pronouns**.

admixture The mixing of elements from one language or dialect into another. This typically happens where speakers are using a variety that is not their native tongue, and where **interference** such as the use of a foreign accent or the **transfer** of grammatical patterns from one language to another takes place. Admixture is an important notion in the study of **pidgin** languages and is one of the major elements in the process of **pidginization**. Admixture can also involve the **borrowing** of words from one language to another.

age-grading A phenomenon in which speakers in a community gradually alter their speech habits as they get older, and where this change is repeated in every generation. It has been shown, for example, that in some speech communities it is normal for speakers to modify their language in the direction of the **acrolect** as they approach middle-age, and then to revert to less prestigious speech patterns after they reach retirement age. Age-grading is something that has to be checked for in **apparent-time studies** of linguistic change to ensure that false conclusions are not being drawn from linguistic differences between generations.

anthrolinguistics see **anthropological linguistics**

anthropological linguistics A branch of the study of language and society, sometimes known as **anthrolinguistics**, in which the objectives of the study are in part identical with those of anthropologists – to find out more about the social structure of particular communities (especially but not exclusively in smaller non-European societies) – but where the methodology involves analysis of languages and of norms for language use. Areas studied in anthropological linguistics include **kinship terminology**, the **Sapir-Whorf hypothesis**, and linguistic **taboo**. There are also strong connections between anthropological linguistics and the **ethnography of speaking**.

antilanguage A variety of a language, usually spoken on particular occasions by members of certain relatively powerless or marginal groups in a society, which is intended to be incomprehensible to other speakers of the language or otherwise to exclude them. Examples of groups employing forms of antilanguage include criminals, drug-users, schoolchildren, homosexuals and gypsies. Exclusivity is maintained through the use of **slang** vocabulary, sometimes known as **argot**, not known to other groups, including vocabulary derived from other languages. European examples include the antilanguage Polari, which is English with a small **admixture** of Romance vocabulary, and Anglo-Romani, which consists of English grammar and pronunciation with vocabulary taken from the (originally north Indian) Gypsy language Romani. Such varieties may rely as well or instead on phonological distortion processes to make them incomprehensible. Examples of this are Cockney back slang, e.g., *yob* = *boy*; London, Glasgow and Australian rhyming slang, e.g., *butchers*, from *butcher's hook* = *look*; and American schoolchildren's Pig Latin, e.g., *ookbay* = *book*.

apparent-time studies Studies of linguistic change which attempt to investigate language changes as they happen, not in real time (see **real-time studies**), but by comparing the speech of older speakers with that of younger speakers in a given community, and assuming that differences between them are due to changes currently taking place within the dialect of that community, with older speakers using older forms and vice versa. As pointed out by William Labov, who introduced both the term and the technique, it is important to be able to distinguish in this comparison of age-groups between ongoing language changes and differences that are due to **age-grading**.

argot see **antilanguage**

artificial languages see **historicity**

Ausbau language (German /'ausbau/) A **variety** which derives its status as a **language**, rather than a **dialect**, not so much from its linguistic characteristics, like an **Abstand language**, but from its social, cultural and political characteristics. These characteristics will normally involve **autonomy** and **standardization**. Norwegian and Swedish are regarded as distinct languages, not because they are linguistically very different from one another – there is clear **mutual intelligibility** – but because they are associated with two separate, independent nation states, and because they have traditions involving different writing systems, grammar books, and dictionaries. **Ausbau** is the German word for 'extension' or 'building up'.

autonomy Independence – the opposite of **heteronomy**. Autonomy is a characteristic of a **variety** of a **language** that has been subject to **standardization** and **codification**, and is therefore regarded as having an independent existence. An autonomous variety is one whose speakers and writers are not socially, culturally, or educationally dependent on any other variety of that language, and is normally the variety which is used in writing in the community in question. **Standard English** is a **dialect** which has the characteristic of autonomy, whereas Cockney does not have this feature.

basilect In a social **dialect continuum**, the **lect** which has the lowest social status. In the Jamaican **post-creole continuum**, the basilect is the variety most unlike the **Standard English acrolect**, namely Jamaican **Creole**. Ranged above the basilect on the continuum are the **mesolects** and the **acrolect**.

bidialectalism (1) The ability of a speaker to command more than one dialect of a language, and to show **code-switching** from one to another depending on **social context**. This ability is more common in **divergent dialect communities**. Most often, bidialectalism involves the ability to use the standard dialect of a language together with some **nonstandard dialect**. (2) An educational policy which is intended to give pupils who are not native-speakers of the standard language writing proficiency in the standard while respecting and helping to maintain their local nonstandard dialects. This policy, which is sometimes known as **bidialectism**, is normal in many countries, e.g., Switzerland, and is the only policy allowed by law in Norway. It is also the educational policy favoured by most sociolinguists involved in mother-tongue education.

bidialectism see **bidialectalism**

bilingualism The ability of an individual to speak two or more languages. In the usage of some writers, bilingualism refers only to individuals who have native command of more than one language. Other writers use the term to refer to any speaker who has a reasonable degree of competence in some language other than their mother tongue. Sociolinguists are agreed that bilingualism is so widespread in the world that there are probably more people in the world who are bilingual, at least in the second sense, than there are monolinguals. Many sociolinguists use the term 'bilingualism' to refer to individuals, even if they are trilingual, quadrilingual, etc., and reserve the term **multilingualism** for nations or societies, even if only two languages are involved.

bioprogram hypothesis A hypothesis proposed by Derek Bickerton and discussed at length in his book *Roots of Language*. Bickerton suggests that humans have a separate biological program for language and that the nature of this innate program is most open for study by linguists in the case of **creole** languages where communities of children have had to develop fully-fledged languages from limited and inadequate **pidgin** language sources. In other language communities, the bioprogram grammar will have been overridden by discourse needs and cultural developments. Creoles have linguistic characteristics in common and these similarities are due to the fact that their grammatical structures are derived directly from the bioprogram without any subsequent cultural overlay. This hypothesis might have implications for the study of the origins of human language.

Black Vernacular English (BVE) The name used by American sociolinguists to refer to the **dialect** of English spoken, with relatively little regional variation, by lower-class Black speakers in the United States. In its phonological and, especially, grammatical characteristics (such as **copula deletion**), this **variety** differs from White dialects of English in such a way that many linguists have argued that it represents a late stage historically in a **decreolization** process of an earlier **creole** that formerly resembled the creoles of the Caribbean. William Labov has argued, in research published in the 1980s, that Black Vernacular English is currently diverging from White dialects. This research has led to the **divergence controversy** in American sociolinguistics.

borrowing The process whereby bilingual speakers introduce words from one language into another language, and these **loan words** eventually become accepted as an integral part of the second language. *Restaurant* was originally a French word, but is now an integral part of the English language, and is known and used by all speakers of English whether or not they are bilingual in French. It is also pronounced by English speakers according to the rules of English and not French pronunciation. Loan words which are still in the process of being assimilated into another language may continue to be pronounced, as well as speakers are able, according to the rules of the original language, as with *coup d'état* in English. Grammatical constructions and speech sounds may also be borrowed from one language into another.

bundles of isoglosses see **transition zone**

BVE see **Black Vernacular English**

change from above In terminology introduced by William Labov, linguistic changes which take place in a community above the level of conscious awareness, i.e. speakers have some awareness that they are making these changes. Very often, changes from above are made as a result of the influence of prestigious dialects with which the community is in contact, and the consequent **stigmatization** of local dialect features. Changes from above therefore typically occur in the first instance in more closely monitored **styles**, and thus lead to **style stratification**. It is important to realize, however, that 'above' in this context does not refer to social class or status. It is not necessarily the case that such changes take place 'from above' socially. Change from above as a process is opposed by Labov to **change from below**.

change from below In terminology introduced by William Labov, linguistic changes which take place in a community below the level of conscious awareness, i.e. speakers are not consciously aware, unlike with **changes from above**, that such changes are taking place. Changes from below usually begin in one particular social class group, and thus lead to **class stratification**. While this particular social class group is very often not the highest class group in a society, it should be noted that change from below does not mean change 'from below' in any social sense.

class stratification A term from **secular linguistics** which refers to the relationship between language and social class, whereby certain variants of a **linguistic variable** are used most often by higher-class speakers, and other variants most frequently by lower-class speakers. Speakers from intermediate classes will use these variants with intermediate frequency, or else will use intermediate variants. Many British communities have class stratification of the variable (t) – the pronunciation of /t/ in *better*, *bet*, etc. – with the variant [t] being used more frequently by higher-class speakers and the variant [ʔ] being used more frequently by lower-class speakers.

classical language A language which has the characteristics of **autonomy** and **standardization** but which does not have the characteristic of **vitality**, i.e. although it used to have native speakers, it no longer does so. Classical European languages include Latin and Ancient Greek. The ancient Indian language Sanskrit, an ancestor of modern North Indian languages such as Hindi and Bengali, is another example of a classical language, as is Classical Arabic. Classical languages generally survive because they are written languages which are known non-natively as a result of being used for purposes of religion or scholarship. Latin has been associated with Catholicism, Sanskrit with Hinduism, and Classical Arabic with Islam.

code-mixing The process whereby speakers indulge in **code-switching** between languages of such rapidity and density, even within sentences and phrases, that it is not really possible to say at any given time which language they are speaking. There are many reports from countries such as Malta, Nigeria and Hong Kong of educated elites indulging in code-mixing, using a mixture of English and the local language. Sociolinguistic explanations for this behaviour normally concentrate on the possibility, through using code-mixing as a strategy, of projecting two identities at once, e.g., that of a modern, sophisticated, educated person *and* that of a loyal, local patriot (see **acts of identity**).

code-switching The process whereby bilingual or bidialectal speakers switch back and forth between one language or dialect and another within the same conversation. This linguistic behaviour is very common in multilingual situations. Sociolinguistic research in this area has concentrated on trying to establish what factors in the social and linguistic context influence switching: it may be that one language is typically associated with one set of **domains**, and the other language with another. Research has also focused on what are the grammatical rules for where switching can and cannot take place, and the extent to which it is possible to distinguish between code-switching and **borrowing**.

codification The process whereby a **variety** of a **language**, often as part of a **standardization** process, acquires a publicly recognized and fixed form, in which norms are laid down for 'correct' usage as far as grammar, vocabulary, spelling and maybe pronunciation are concerned. This codification can take place over time without involvement of official bodies, as happened with **Standard English**, or it can take place quite rapidly, as a result of conscious decisions by governmental or other official planning agencies, as happened with Swahili in Tanzania. The results of codification are usually enshrined in dictionaries and grammar books, as well as, sometimes, in government publications.

communicative competence A term introduced by the American anthropological linguist Dell Hymes by analogy with Chomsky's term **competence** – the native speaker's (unconscious) linguistic knowledge of the structure of his or her language. Hymes points out that knowing the grammar, phonology, and lexicon of a language is not enough. All native speakers of a language also have to know how to *use* that language appropriately in the society in which they live. They have to know when to speak and when not to, which greeting formula to use when, which style to use in which situation, and so on. Non-native speakers also have to acquire communicative as well as linguistic competence when learning a foreign language, if they are to be able to use that language effectively and appropriately and participate in **cross-cultural communication**. The **ethnography of speaking** involves the study of what is necessary to be communicatively competent in different communities.

competence see **communicative competence**

complication The process associated with **decreolization** and **depidginization** in which the **simplification** which has taken place during **pidginization** is 'repaired' as a result of **language contact** between the **creole** or **pidgin** and the **source language**. Complication thus takes the form of the reintroduction of irregularities, etc., that are present in the source language but absent in the creole or pidgin.

constraints In **variation theory**, linguistic and social factors which have been shown to influence linguistic variation. For instance, the simplification of consonant clusters in English, as in *old* > *ol'*, *left* > *lef'*, *west* > *wes'*, is variable: most speakers sometimes simplify these clusters and sometimes do not. This variation, however, is not random (although one can never predict in any given instance whether it will occur or not). The probability that a consonant cluster will be simplified depends on a number of factors which influence or constrain this variability. There are phonological constraints, with simplification being more frequent before consonants, as in *west side*, than before vowels, as in *west end*; grammatical constraints, with simplification being less frequent where grammatical endings are involved, as in *left them*, than where they are not, as in *left side*; and stylistic constraints, with simplification being more frequent in informal than in formal situations.

convergence see **accommodation**

conversation analysis An area of sociolinguistics with links to ethnomethodology which analyses the structure and norms of conversation in **face-to-face interaction**. Conversation analysts look at aspects of conversation such as the relationship between questions and answers, or summonses and responses. They are also concerned with rules for conversational discourse, such as those involving **turn-taking**; with conversational devices such as **discourse markers**; and with norms for participating in conversation, such as what are the rules for interruption, for changing topic, for overlapping between one speaker and another, for remaining silent, for closing a conversation, and so on. In so far as norms for conversational interaction may vary from society to society, conversation analysis may also have links with **cross-cultural communication** and the **ethnography of speaking**. By some writers it is opposed to **discourse analysis**.

copula absence see **copula deletion**

copula deletion A feature of a number of **dialects** of English, notably American **Black Vernacular English**. In these dialects, forms of the copula (the verb *to be*) are variably absent in certain grammatical and phonological contexts. Thus it is grammatical in these dialects to say *He nice* or *We coming* or *She a teacher*, but not, for example, **I know who you*. Many **creole** languages also lack the copula in these positions, as do many non-creole languages such as Russian and Hungarian, but since this is not a variable feature of these languages, it is better to refer in these cases to **copula absence** rather than 'copula deletion'.

corpus planning An aspect of **language planning** and **codification** in which decisions are taken about the linguistic characteristics of the variety of language in question. Typical corpus planning issues involve questions concerning which pronunciation to use of those available; which syntactic structures and morphological forms are to be permitted; which of a number of regionally based words of identical meaning is to be favoured; and what is to be done about expansion of the vocabulary, if this is thought to be necessary. Corpus planning is usually contrasted with **status planning**. (See also **language development.**)

correctness In **speech communities** which have been subject to considerable focusing (see **focused**), native speakers tend to have notions about which linguistic forms are correct and which are not. Linguists agree that the language of non-native speakers can be labelled 'incorrect' if it contains constructions or usages that would never be employed by native speakers, such as *I am knowing him since many years*. They do not agree, however, that judgements about correctness can legitimately be made about forms used by native speakers. They point out that when such judgements are made about forms in widespread use, such as *I done it*, they are essentially social judgements which have to do with the distribution of power, wealth and prestige in a community.

correlational sociolinguistics A term applied by some writers to the work of linguists like William Labov who in their research have correlated **linguistic variables** with social parameters such as sex, age and social class. The term, however, is never used by the practitioners of this type of work, and should be avoided in favour of other terms such as **secular linguistics**, since it implies that the correlation is central and an end in itself rather than what it actually is, namely a means to an end – a methodology for studying phenomena such as linguistic change.

covert prestige A term introduced by William Labov in his 1966 book *The Social Stratification of English in New York City* to refer to the favourable connotations that nonstandard or apparently low-status or 'incorrect' forms have for many speakers. Standard words, pronunciations and grammatical forms have overt prestige in that they are publicly acknowledged as 'correct' and as bestowing high social status on their users. We have to assume, however, that nonstandard and apparently low-status forms do also have a kind of less publicly acknowledged or hidden prestige which leads their users to continue to use them. The covert prestige associated with such linguistic forms bestows status on their users as being members of their local community, and as having desirable qualities such as friendliness and loyalty.

creole A language which has undergone considerable **pidginization** but where the **reduction** associated with pidginization has been repaired by a process of **expansion** or creolization, as a result of its having acquired a community of native speakers, and of being employed for an increasingly wide range of purposes. Creoles which have not undergone any **decreolization** are not normally intelligible to speakers of the original **source language**. Some of the better-known creoles include English-based creoles like the Sranan of Surinam, French-based creoles such as Haitian Creole, and Portuguese-based creoles such as that of the Cape Verde Islands, but by no means all of them are based on European languages. It is a common but undesirable practice to refer to any language which has undergone **admixture** as a creole. (See also **bioprogram hypothesis**.)

creolization see **creole**

creoloid A language which, as a result of **language contact**, has experienced **simplification** and **admixture**, but has not undergone the **reduction** associated with full pidginization (nor, therefore, the **expansion** associated with creolization). Such a language will resemble in its linguistic characteristics a **creole** which has undergone **decreolization**, but will be different in its history: a creoloid remains at all times intelligible to speakers of its **source language** if this remains separate from the creoloid; and it maintains throughout its development a community of native speakers. A good example of a creoloid is the South African language Afrikaans, which is historically a form of Dutch which has undergone a certain amount of **simplification** and **admixture** in a multilingual contact situation. Some writers have argued that English is in origin a creoloid: a simplified, mixed form of Old English that arose in the Old English–Norman French–Old Norse contact situation.

cross-cultural communication Communication between speakers from different cultural backgrounds, which can often be difficult because of different assumptions about when, why and how language is to be used. As demonstrated by the **ethnography of speaking**, different communities have different norms for how language is to be employed. Cross-cultural communication does not necessarily imply that different languages are involved. Speakers of Australian English whose families are of Greek origin, for example, have been shown to have different ideas about the use of irony than speakers of the same language who are of British Isles origin.

dachlos see **roofless dialects**

decreolization A situation which arises when a **creole** language remains or comes back into contact with its original **source**

language, and is influenced linguistically by the source language if, as is often the case, the source language has higher prestige. Speakers of the creole will accommodate (see **accommodation**) to the source language, and the creole will become more like the source language. The original **pidginization**, which led to the development of the pidgin precursor of the creole, involved the processes of **reduction**, **simplification** and **admixture**. The reduction will already have been 'repaired' by the process of **expansion** during creolization. Decreolization thus consists linguistically of two processes, one which counteracts the simplification, namely **complication**, and another which removes the admixture, namely **purification**. Decreolization often leads to the development of a **post-creole continuum**.

dense see **network strength**

depidginization The linguistic processes of **complication**, **purification** (see **decreolization**) and **expansion**, by which a **pidgin** or pidginized (see **pidginization**) **variety** of language comes to resemble or become identical with the **source language** from which it was originally derived. This may occur if speakers of the pidgin or pidginized variety have extensive contacts with speakers of the source language.

determination see **language determination**; **status planning**

development see **language development**

dialect A **variety** of language which differs grammatically, phonologically and lexically from other varieties, and which is associated with a particular geographical area and/or with a particular social class or status group (see also **sociolect**). Varieties which differ from one another only in pronunciation are known as **accents**. Varieties which are associated only with particular social situations are known as **styles**. Neither of these should be confused with dialect. The term is often used to refer only to **nonstandard dialects** or to **traditional dialects**. Strictly speaking, however, standard varieties such as **Standard English** are just as much dialects as any other dialect. A **language** is typically composed of a number of dialects.

dialect area see **transition zone**

dialect contact Contact between linguistic **varieties** which results from communication between speakers of different but **mutually intelligible** dialects, often involving **accommodation**. Such communication is of course very common indeed, but, from the point of view of sociolinguistics, such contacts are particularly interesting where they occur on a large scale, such as at dialect boundaries (see **isogloss**) or as a result of urbanization or colonization. In these cases, phenomena such as **dialect mixture** and **hyperadaptation** may occur.

dialect continuum (plural: **continua**) A very common situation in which geographically neighbouring dialects, particularly **traditional** rural **dialects**, differ from one another minimally but in which the further one travels from any starting point the more different dialects become. All dialects will be intelligible to speakers of neighbouring dialects, but the greater the distance between locations where dialects are spoken, the more difficult comprehension will be. If the geographical area in question is large enough, dialects which are linked to one another by a chain of mutual intelligibility of intervening dialects may nevertheless themselves not be mutually intelligible. The Low German dialects of Schleswig-Holstein, northern Germany, are part of the same dialect continuum as the Swiss German dialects of central Switzerland, and are linked to them by a chain of mutual intelligibility – there is nowhere on the continuum where speakers cannot understand the dialects of neighbouring villages – but they are not mutually intelligible. Dialect continua can also be **social**, with **sociolects** changing gradually as one moves up or down the social scale. (See also **acrolect**; **mesolect**; **basilect**.)

dialect mixture A consequence of large-scale, long-term **dialect contact** in which **face-to-face interaction** between speakers of different dialects, stemming from developments such as emigration or urbanization, leads to **accommodation** between these speakers and thus the mixing of different **dialect** forms. The end result of the mixture may ultimately be the formation of a new dialect, such as Australian English, with speakers selecting a combination of forms from different dialects which are present in the mixture for retention, and discarding others. The new dialect will typically have the linguistic characteristics of a **koiné**.

dialectology The academic study of dialects, often associated especially with the phonological, morphological and lexical study of rural **traditional dialects**, which were the original concern of this discipline, and the spatial or geographical distribution of traditional dialect forms (see **traditional dialectology**). In more recent years, however, dialectologists have also been concerned with syntactic features, with **urban dialectology**, with **social dialectology**, and with the social distribution of linguistic forms (see **sociolects**).

dialectometry A form of spatial **dialectology**, which has links with **geolinguistics** (1) and with **traditional dialectology**. Dialectometry is associated particularly with the work of Jean Séguy, and involves the study of (for the most part) **traditional dialects** using quantitative and computerized methodology for the location and weighting of **isoglosses**.

dialect-switching see **divergent dialect community**

diffuse According to a typology of language varieties developed by the British sociolinguist Robert B. LePage, a characteristic of certain language communities, and thus language varieties. Some communities are relatively more diffuse, while others are relatively more **focused**. Any speech act performed by an individual constitutes an **act of identity**. If a wide range of identities is available for enactment in a **speech community**, that community can be regarded as diffuse. Diffuse linguistic communities tend to be those where little **standardization** or **codification** have taken place, where there is relatively little agreement about norms of usage, where speakers show little concern for marking their language variety off from other varieties, and where they may accord relatively little importance even to what their language is called.

diffusion (1) The process whereby words, pronunciations or grammatical forms spread or diffuse from one variety to another. To do this, forms must spread from one speaker to another via **face-to-face interaction** in situations of **dialect contact**, in which speakers of different dialects may **accommodate** to each other and, if interaction is frequent enough, permanently acquire features from other dialects. Diffusion may be geographical, in which forms spread from one area (and thus geographical dialect) to another, or social, in which forms spread from one social group (and thus **sociolect**) to another. 'Diffusion' can also be used of the geographical spread of a **language**, often at the expense of another through **language shift**, or as a result of **language planning**. (2) The carrying out of **speech acts** and other processes whereby speech communities become **diffuse**, in the sense of LePage.

diglossia (1) A term associated with the American linguist Charles A. Ferguson describing sociolinguistic situations such as those that obtain in Arabic-speaking countries and in German-speaking Switzerland. In such a diglossic community, the prestigious standard or 'High' (or H) **variety**, which is linguistically related to but significantly different from the **vernacular** or 'Low' (or L) **varieties**, has no native speakers. All members of the speech community are native speakers of one of the L varieties, such as Colloquial Arabic and Swiss German, and learn the H variety, such as Classical Arabic and Standard German, at school. H varieties are typically used in writing and in high status spoken **domains** where preparation of what is to be said or read is possible. L varieties are used in all other contexts. (2) Ferguson's original term was later extended by the American sociolinguist Joshua Fishman to include sociolinguistic situations other than those where the H and L varieties are varieties of the same language, such as Arabic or German. In Fishman's usage, even multilingual countries such as Nigeria, where English functions as a nation-wide prestige language which is learnt in school and local languages such as Hausa and Yoruba are spoken natively, are described as being diglossic. In these cases, languages such as English are described as H varieties, and languages such as Yoruba as L.

discourse analysis A branch of linguistics which deals with linguistic units at levels above the sentence, i.e. texts and conversations. Those branches of discourse analysis which come under the heading of language and society presuppose that language is being used in social interaction and thus deal with conversation. Other non-sociolinguistic branches of discourse analysis are often known as **text linguistics**. Discourse analysis is opposed by some writers, to **conversation analysis**.

discourse marker Units recognized by linguists working in **conversation analysis** and **discourse analysis**. Discourse markers are words, phrases or sounds which have no real lexical meaning but have instead an important function in marking conversational structure, in signalling the conversational intentions of speakers, and in securing co-operation and responses from listeners. Discourse markers in English include *well*, *oh*, *actually*, *OK*, *now*, and so on.

distance see **Abstand language**

divergence see **accommodation**

divergence controversy A controversy between certain American linguists about the relationship between **Black Vernacular English** and other varieties of American English. It is generally agreed amongst American linguists that BVE has converged on White varieties of English over the centuries, i.e. it is now more similar to White dialects than it used to be, and may even be a decreolized **creole**. However, data obtained by sociolinguists from the 1980s has been interpreted by some as indicating that it is once again diverging from White varieties, perhaps as a result of the increasing ghettoization and residential separation of White and Black Americans. Other linguists disagree with this analysis, and dispute the data and/or its interpretation.

divergent dialect community A **speech community** in which the **vernacular variety** is linguistically very different from the prestige or standard variety. In such communities, there may exist a very long social **dialect continuum**, such as a **post-creole continuum**. Alternatively, if no such continuum exists, the clear linguistic separation of vernacular and standard may lead to **code-switching** or dialect-switching between the varieties. Diglossic communities (see

diglossia [1]) are a special case of divergent dialect communities. Sociolinguists encounter different methodological problems in divergent dialect communities than in other communities, particularly in the setting up of **linguistic variables**. Within the English-speaking world, divergent dialect communities are to be found in the Caribbean and in northern Britain and northern Ireland. Communities in North America and southern England (except for speakers of **traditional dialects**) typically speak dialects which are linguistically much more similar to **Standard English**.

domain A concept employed particularly in studies of **code-switching** in multilingual contexts and in the study of other situations where different **languages**, **dialects** or **styles** are used in different **social contexts**. A domain is a combination of factors which are believed to influence choice of code (language, dialect or style) by speakers. Such factors might include participants (in a conversation), topic and location. For example, the domestic domain, which would probably produce an informal style of speech, might involve the home location, family participants and a day-to-day topic.

domestic domain see **domain**

double negative see **multiple negation**

elaborated code A concept developed by the British sociologist Basil Bernstein in connection with his work on language use, social class and socialization. Elaborated code, originally called 'public language', is a form of language use which, according to Bernstein, is characterized by a high degree of explicitness, and is therefore suitable for public use in situations where participants do not have a large fund of shared knowledge or assumptions in common. Elaborated code is thought of as lying at the opposite end of a continuum of types of language use from **restricted code**. Bernstein argued that some working-class children in Britain were disadvantaged in the education system because they were unable to use elaborated code. Bernstein's theory aroused considerable hostility on the part of linguists in its initial formulation as it discussed – irrelevantly, as it now seems – grammatical features, such as pronouns and relative clauses, and was interpreted by some educationists as having some link to **Standard English**. Elaborated code in fact has no connection with any **dialect**, but is rather concerned, as part of a theory of **language use** and social structure, with the content of what speakers say.

embedding problem One of a number of problems pointed to by the American sociolinguist William Labov in connection with the study of linguistic change within the field of **secular linguistics**. It is the problem, in the study of linguistic changes as they are actually taking place, of locating and analysing both the linguistic and social settings in which the changes are occurring. In the study of sound change, the linguist not only has to look at structural pressures in the sound system, as was the practice in pre-Labovian historical linguistics, but also – and simultaneously – at the social background against which the change is taking place. The change has to be situated in a matrix of both linguistic and social factors.

ethnic group An important concept both in **language planning** studies and in certain types of **secular linguistics**. An ethnic group is a sociocultural group or 'race' of people who feel themselves to be members of a social entity which is distinct from other social groups and with a culture that is distinct from that of other groups. As defined by the American sociolinguist Joshua Fishman, an ethnic group is smaller and more locality-bound than a **nationality**, but this distinction is not maintained by all writers. There is in any case a continuum of size and locality-boundedness along which groups of people can be ranged. Thus it is not unusual for groups as different in size – and relative size within their own nation (see **nationism**) – as Black Americans, Scandinavian Sami, Icelanders, and Ukrainians to be referred to as constituting ethnic groups.

ethnography of communication A term identical in reference to **ethnography of speaking**, except that nonverbal communication is also included. For example, proxemics – the study of factors such as how physically close to each other speakers may be, in different cultures, when communicating with one another – could be discussed under this heading.

ethnography of speaking A branch of sociolinguistics or anthropological linguistics particularly associated with the American scholar Dell Hymes. The ethnography of speaking studies the norms and rules for using language in social situations in different cultures and is thus clearly important for **cross-cultural communication**. The concept of **communicative competence** is a central one in the ethnography of speaking. Central topics include the study of who is allowed to speak to who – and when; what types of language are to be used in different contexts; how to do things with language, such as make requests or tell jokes; how much **indirectness** it is normal to employ; how often it is usual to speak, and how much one should say; how long it is permitted to remain silent; and the use of formulaic language such as expressions used for greeting, leave-taking and thanking.

ethnomethodology A branch of sociology which has links with certain sorts of sociolinguistics such as **conversation analysis** because of its use of recorded conversational material as data. Most ethnomethodologists, however, are generally not interested in the language of conversation as such but rather in the content of what is said. They study, not language or speech, but **talk**. In particular, they are interested in what is *not* said. They focus on the shared common-sense knowledge speakers have of their society which they can leave unstated in conversation because it is taken for granted by all participants.

expansion Part of the process of **creolization** in which the **reduction** which has occurred during **pidginization** is repaired, as the **creole** acquires native speakers and/or is used in a wider range of functions. Expansion involves an increase in the vocabulary of the language, as well as the development of an often much wider range of grammatical and stylistic devices. Sometimes this development may take place with the help of external stimuli, such as when words are borrowed from other languages. Other developments may be language-internal, such as when new words are coined, by compounding or some other means, from words already available in the language. As far as grammatical expansion is concerned, it is the development of grammatical categories and devices without external stimuli that is the focus of the **bioprogram hypothesis**, the interest centring on the possibility that new features are generated directly from the innate human language faculty itself.

face In a conversation, speakers' face consists of the positive impression of themselves that they wish to make on the other participants. If such an impression is not successfully conveyed or is not accepted by the other participants, **loss of face** will result. Face, however, is not the sole responsibility of the individual concerned. In many forms of **face-to-face interaction**, all participants will be concerned to maintain not only their own face but also that of the others. (See also **negative politeness** and **positive politeness**.)

face-to-face interaction Conversation or communication between two or more people which is interactive (e.g., it is not a monologue), and in which the participants are physically present (e.g., they are not talking on the telephone). Studies of face-to-face interaction are important in the **social psychology of language**; **conversation analysis**; studies of **positive** and **negative politeness**; and in studies of **accommodation** and **diffusion**.

familiar forms see **T and V pronouns**

fine stratification In Labovian **secular linguistics, linguistic variables** are employed to investigate **social stratification** and **style stratification**. This stratification can take the form of fine stratification or **sharp stratification**. In fine stratification, the correlation reveals a gradient or continuum, with no sharp break in linguistic behaviour, and thus in scores for linguistic variables, between one social group or style and another.

focal area A concept from **traditional dialectology** and more recent work in **dialectometry**, **geolinguistics** (1), and spatial **dialectology**. Traditional dialectologists discovered early on in the history of the discipline that **isoglosses** for individual words and pronunciations rarely coincided with each other. One reaction to that finding was to suggest that there was no such thing as a dialect totally distinct from other dialects. This is in most cases strictly-speaking correct (see **dialect continuum**), but it is not simply the case that isoglosses are randomly distributed. Dialect features show different types of geographical patterning. Some geographical areas are crossed by no or relatively few isoglosses. These are central focal areas or **kernel areas** from which linguistic innovations have spread to surrounding areas. Such focal areas are in turn surrounded by **transition zones** which separate them from other focal areas. Focal areas often centre on influential urban areas or on means of communication such as roads or rivers.

focused According to a typology of language varieties developed by the British sociolinguist Robert B. LePage, some language communities and thus language varieties are relatively more **diffuse**, while others are relatively more focused. Any speech act performed by an individual constitutes an **act of identity**. If only a narrow range of identities is available for enactment in a **speech community**, that community can be regarded as focused. Focused linguistic communities tend to be those where considerable **standardization** and **codification** have taken place, where there is a high degree of agreement about norms of usage, where speakers tend to show concern for 'purity' and marking their language variety off from other varieties, and where everyone agrees about what the language is called. European language communities tend to be heavily focused. LePage points out that notions such as **admixture**, **code-mixing**, **code-switching** and **multilingualism** depend on a focused-language-centred point of view of the separate status of language varieties.

foreigner talk A way of talking to foreigners, or, better, non-native speakers, who are not able – or who are thought not to be able – to understand normal fluent speech in a particular **language**. This term is particularly useful for describing aspects of the language used to foreigners which are **institutionalized**, i.e. there are norms in the language community, which are learned by people growing up in that community, for how one should speak to non-native speakers. These norms may include grammatical **simplification** such as *Me go, you stay* and the use of certain words (such as English *savvy?*) which may well not be known to foreigners at all. Foreigner talk is thought by many to be of interest in the formation of **pidgins**.

formal forms see **T and V pronouns**

genderlect A **variety** or **lect** which is specific to or particularly associated with male or female speakers. This term is in most usages misleading, in that it suggests that there may be communities where male and female speakers use radically different varieties. In fact, while there are some more-or-less gender specific usages in many if not most languages, these range from the use of a small number of words, phrases or conversational devices in some languages to particular vowels, consonants or grammatical endings in others. Most differences between male and female speech are quantitatively revealed tendencies rather than absolute differences.

generic pronoun In linguistics, a generic form is one which refers to a class or group of entities rather than to a specific member of a class. A particular issue in recent discussion about language and society has been the generic use of the English masculine pronouns *he*, *him* and *his* (and similar pronouns in certain other languages) to include both male and female referents, as in *Any student who fails to complete his work* . . ., where students may be either male or female. Feminine pronouns have traditionally not been employed in this generic way, with *she*, *her*, *hers* referring only to female persons. This apparent bias in favour of males can be awkward, illogical or misleading, and it has been argued that the generic use of *he* is unjust and undesirable in societies which believe in the equality of men and women, and linguistic solutions have been sought to the problem, such as the use of the already well-established singular *they* in English (*Any student who fails to complete their work* . . .), the use of written *s/he*, the use of generic *she*, or the invention of totally new pronoun forms.

geography of language see **geolinguistics**

geolinguistics (1) A relatively recent label used by some linguists to refer to work in sociolinguistics which represents a synthesis of Labovian **secular linguistics** and spatial **dialectology**. The quantitative study of the geographical diffusion of words or pronunciations from one area to another is an example of work in this field. (2) A term used by human geographers to describe modern quantitative research on geographical aspects of **language maintenance** and **language shift**, and other aspects of the spatial relationships to be found between languages and dialects. An example of such work is the study of geographical patterning in the use of English and Welsh in Wales. Given the model of the distinction between **sociolinguistics** and the **sociology of language**, it might be better to refer to this sort of work as the **geography of language**.

graphization A term from **language planning** used to describe that part of the process of **language development** which involves the selection of a writing system or alphabet for a language and the agreement on conventions for its orthography or spelling and punctuation. The development of an orthography usually follows on from phonological analysis carried out by linguists.

heteronomy Dependence – the opposite of **autonomy**. Heteronomy is a characteristic of a **variety** of a **language** that has not been subject to **standardization**, and which is not regarded as having an existence independent of a corresponding autonomous standard. A heteronomous variety is typically a nonstandard variety whose speakers and writers are socially, culturally and educationally dependent on an autonomous variety of the same language, and who look to the standard autonomous variety as the one which naturally corresponds to their **vernacular**.

historicity A characteristic of a language or language variety where there is a continuous tradition of native-speakers handing down the language from one generation to another. Languages which do not have this social characteristic include **artificial languages** such as Esperanto; **classical languages**, such as Latin and Sanskrit, which no longer have native speakers; and **pidgin** languages, which do not (yet) have any native speakers.

hyperadaptation A linguistic process resulting from **dialect contact**. Speakers of one **variety** attempt to adopt features from another variety, but overdo it, overgeneralizing from correspondences they have noticed between the two varieties. Thus speakers of non-rhotic English English accents, in attempting to imitate **rhotic** (say, American) **accents**, may incorrectly insert an *r* into the pronunciation of words like *calm* /kɑːm/ > /kɑːrm/ because they have observed that rhotic accents have an *r* in words like *farm* /fɑːrm/ corresponding to their own pronunciation /fɑːm/. The best known term relating to types of hyperadaptation is **hypercorrection**. Other forms include **hyperdialectism**; and **hyperurbanism**, in which speakers of rural dialects overgeneralize urban dialect forms. Linguistically, this process is the same as that which in child language studies and second language learning is called **overgeneralization**.

hypercorrection A form of **hyperadaptation** in which speakers of a lower prestige variety, in attempting to adopt features of a higher prestige variety, incorrectly analyse differences between the two varieties and overgeneralize on the basis of observed correspondences. An example from English English is the faulty 'correction' of the north of England pronunciation of words such as *look* from /lʊk/to supposedly **RP** /lʌk/ by analogy with correctly observed northern versus RP correspondences such as *duck* /dʊk/ versus /dʌk/. (See also **Labov-hypercorrection**.)

hyperdialectism A form of **hyperadaptation** in which speakers produce overgeneralized forms in nonstandard dialects. This can take place as a result of faulty analyses, for example, in the speech of actors attempting to imitate certain regional varieties, and even in the speech of local-dialect speakers themselves if they attempt to reproduce pronunciations or constructions typical of older forms of the dialect with which they are not sufficiently familiar. It can also occur as the result of **neighbour opposition**, when dialect speakers overgeneralize differences between their own and neighbouring dialects in order to symbolize their separate identities.

hyperurbanism see **hyperadaptation**

implicational scale A term from **variation theory** particularly associated with the study of the **post-creole continuum**. The American linguist David DeCamp in 1971 introduced the **implicational table** or scalogram as a way of showing relationships between linguistic varieties. He demonstrated that certain linguistic forms from the Jamaican **social dialect continuum** had both **creole** and **standard** variants. These variants can be ranked in terms of their 'creoleness' and 'standardness' on an implicational hierarchy that is observed by (nearly all) speakers, such that usage by a speaker of creole forms from a particular point on the hierarchy *implies* that one can predict that s/he will also use creole forms from lower down on the hierarchy, but not necessarily from higher up. That is, some mesolectal forms are more basilectal or acrolectal than others. Similarly, use of standard forms from a particular point on the continuum implies also use of standard forms from higher up on the hierarchy, but not necessarily of those from lower down. (See also **lect**.)

implicational table A table used to portray implicational relation-

Speaker	*Feature*				
	1	*2*	*3*	*4*	*5*
A	*Standard*	*Standard*	*Standard*	*Standard*	*Standard*
B	*Standard*	*Standard*	*Standard*	*Standard*	*Creole*
C	*Standard*	*Standard*	*Standard*	*Creole*	*Creole*
D	*Standard*	*Standard*	*Creole*	*Creole*	*Creole*
E	*Standard*	*Creole*	*Creole*	*Creole*	*Creole*
F	*Creole*	*Creole*	*Creole*	*Creole*	*Creole*

Fig. 1 Implicational table

ships, such as those obtaining on a **post-creole** or other **social dialect continuum**, between speakers' use of linguistic features, in which variants can be ranged on an **implicational scale**, as in Fig. 1.

impoverishment see **reduction**

indicator In **secular linguistics**, a **linguistic variable** which shows **social stratification** but not **style stratification**. In investigations of the **embedding problem** associated with linguistic change, indicators represent a relatively early stage in the development of linguistic variables, and may later on develop into **markers**. Indicators are typically involved in **change from below**.

indirectness A term particularly associated with **conversation analysis** and the **ethnography of speaking**. It is normal in all human societies for speakers not always to say exactly what they mean. It is important for reasons to do with **face** and **negative** and **positive politeness** that speakers should on some occasions be able to hint at their meanings rather than stating them directly. The American sociolinguist Deborah Tannen has argued that some societies use this sort of indirectness as a conversational strategy more frequently than others. In communities such as Greece, where indirectness is rather frequently employed, speakers will thus be more sensitive to hints and clues as to what speakers' true intentions and feeling are than in, for example, many English-speaking cultures. She has also suggested that American men use indirectness less, and are therefore less sensitive to its use by others, than American women.

inherent variability A term from **secular linguistics** which is employed to claim that variability in a particular **language variety** is not the result of the **borrowing** of additional variants from other varieties but is inherent in the system of the variety itself. While it is acknowledged that borrowing from other varieties does occur, it is also agreed by sociolinguists that all dialects of all languages are inherently variable to some extent: variability is a universal characteristic of human language. Variability may be related to an ongoing linguistic change, with variation occurring between older and newer forms, but this is not necessarily the case. Many varieties of British English, for example, show inherent variability in alternation between /h/ and ∅ in words such as *hat*, *house* and *hedge* (see **linguistic variable**) which is not involved in any current linguistic change at all.

institutionalized see **foreigner talk**; **lingua franca**

intellectualization The process in **language planning** in which the vocabulary of the **language** of a community is expanded, either by **borrowing** from other languages or by coining, compounding or other language-internal means. Intellectualization is undertaken in order to enable a language's speakers more readily to speak and write about academic, scientific and other topics which the community has hitherto not spoken or written about, or which it has spoken and written about using some other language.

interference see **admixture**

isogloss A term from **dialectology** for a line drawn on a dialect map marking off an area which has one particular variant of a linguistic form from another neighbouring area which has a different variant. An additional term **isophone** is available in strict usage for referring to lines drawn between areas which have different phonetic or phonological variants, leaving isogloss to refer to lexical differences. In practice, however, most writers use isogloss to apply to phonetic, phonological, grammatical *and* lexical boundaries. Well-known isoglosses include the *maken–machen* line in Germany, the *path* /pæθ/–/pɑːθ/ line in England, and the *greasy* /s/–/z/ line in the USA.

isophone see **isogloss**

jargon (1) A form of **language** which has arisen in a **language contact** situation as a result of **pidginization**, but which has not yet undergone **stabilization** or focusing (see **focused**) or any form of even informal **codification**. Such **diffuse** language varieties are also known as **pre-pidgin varieties**. (2) A non-technical term used of the **register** associated with a particular activity by outsiders who do not participate in this activity. The use of this term implies that one considers the vocabulary of the register in question to be unnecessarily difficult and obscure. The register of law may be referred to as 'legal jargon' by non-lawyers.

kernel area see **focal area**

kinship terminology Terms used to label the family relationships in human society. All human societies have the same family relationships, contracted through birth and marriage, in common. Different societies, however, group these relationships together and label them in linguistically different ways. The study of the words used to label such relationships in different societies is thus of both semantic and anthropological interest. English-speaking people do not distinguish linguistically between *uncle* 'father's brother', 'mother's brother', 'father's sister's husband', and 'mother's sister's husband'. Certain other languages do distinguish between all or some of these different relationships, and/or group them together with other relationships which in English are separate from *uncle*: 'father' and 'father's brother' may share the same term, for instance. The assumption is that this differential linguistic labelling reflects differences in the structures of different societies and in the roles and behaviour which are expected of individuals having particular relationships with one another.

koiné A linguistic variety which has grown up in a **dialect contact** situation as a result of **koinéization**. The process of koinéization consists of **dialect mixture** together with or followed by the processes of **levelling** and **simplification**. The word 'koiné' is the Ancient Greek word for 'common'. Urban dialects are often koinés based on a mixture of original rural dialects; and **standard languages** may also be varieties that have undergone certain amounts of koinéization.

koinéization see **koiné**; **simplification**; **traditional dialect**

Labov-hypercorrection A secular linguistic term associated with the **embedding problem** in which **style stratification** of **markers** is such that (usually) the second highest status group in a **speech community** uses higher-status variants in formal styles more frequently than the highest status group. This linguistic behaviour can be interpreted as being the result of **linguistic insecurity**. Labov-hypercorrection should be distinguished from **hypercorrection**, which is a feature of the speech of individuals. Labov-hypercorrection is a term which is due to the British linguist J. C. Wells, who suggested that it was necessary to distinguish terminologically between individual hypercorrection, and group hypercorrection of the type first described by William Labov in his research in New York City.

Labovian sociolinguistics Another term for **secular linguistics**. The American linguist William Labov is the leading figure in this field and pioneered work of this type, notably in his 1966 publication, *The Social Stratification of English in New York City*.

lame A term introduced into sociolinguistics from **Black Vernacular English** by William Labov, and now used as a technical term to describe individuals who are 'outsiders' or only peripheral members of a particular **social network** or **peer group**. It is believed that the linguistic behaviour of lames is less regular, because it is less subject to focusing (see **focused**), than that of core members of a group. Labov also points out that academic linguists typically are – or have become – lames, and that their intuitions about their own original dialects may therefore be somewhat unreliable.

language Not only a linguistic but also a political, cultural, social and historical term. An **Ausbau**-type language is a collection of linguistic varieties which consists of an autonomous variety, together with all the varieties that are heteronomous (dependent) on it. Whether or not a group of varieties form an Ausbau type of language will be doubtful, or impossible to determine, where none of the varieties is autonomous. This will also be difficult in situations where the nature or direction of heteronomy is a matter of political or cultural dispute. There are thus disagreements as to whether Serbo-Croat is one or two languages (see **polycentric standard**); whether Macedonian is a language in its own right or a dialect of Bulgarian; whether Sami (Lappish) is one language or six; and so on. **Abstand**-type languages can be considered languages for purely linguistic reasons.

language attitudes The attitudes which people have towards different **languages**, **dialects**, **accents**, and their speakers. Such attitudes may range from very favourable to very unfavourable, and may be manifested in subjective judgements about the 'correctness', worth, and aesthetic qualities of varieties, as well as about the personal qualities of their speakers. Linguistics has shown that such attitudes have no linguistic basis. Sociolinguistics notes that such attitudes are social in origin, but that they may have important effects on language behaviour, being involved in **acts of identity**, and on linguistic change (see **linguistic insecurity**). Language attitudes is one of the most important topics in the **social psychology of language**.

language conflict In multilingual situations, social strife and other problems which arise where the needs or rights or wishes of different groups speaking different languages conflict. The term is more especially applied to disagreements that are specifically to do with language, such as which language is to be the official language in a particular area; which language are children to get their education in; and which language is to be used in the courts. Belgium has a history of language conflict, with disagreements concerning language-use rights between its Dutch-, French- and German-speaking populations flaring up from time to time. **Language planning** activities are often directed at solving problems arising out of language conflict.

language contact A term used to apply to situations where two or more groups of speakers who do not have a native language in common are in social contact with one another or come into such contact. Communication between the groups may be difficult in the short term, and may in the long term lead to the different languages influencing one another, as a result of **bilingualism** on the part of (some of) the speakers involved. Language contact may lead to or involve phenomena such as **borrowing**, **code-switching**, **language shift**, **lingua francas**, **multilingualism**, and **pidginization**. (See also **dialect contact**.)

language cultivation A term often used to translate Scandinavian *språkvård*. Its meaning is roughly equivalent to **language development** or **corpus planning**, but it is also concerned, as they are not, with notions such as **correctness** and literary style.

language death In situations of **multilingualism** and **language contact**, **language shift** may take place, particularly on the part of **linguistic minority** groups. If the entire community shifts totally to a new language, the original language will eventually have no speakers left in the community in question, and the end point of the process of language shift will be language death. Some writers distinguish between situations of **language loss**, where total shift occurs in only one of the communities speaking the language, such as the loss of Dutch in immigrant communities in Australia; and language death, which is the total loss of a language from the world, when all the speakers of a language shift, as with the loss of Manx on the Isle of Man. We can also distinguish **language murder**, when a language dies out as a result of genocide, as in the case of Tasmanian. (See also **language endangerment**.)

language deficit see **verbal deprivation**

language determination A term from **language planning** not significantly different in its usage from **status planning**.

language development In **language planning**, language development consists of the processes of **graphization**, **standardization**, and **intellectualization**. (See also **corpus planning.**)

language endangerment A situation in which a language is in danger of undergoing **language death**.

language loss see **language death**

language maintenance The opposite of **language shift** and **language death**. Where language maintenance occurs, a community of speakers continues speaking its original language, rather than shifting to some other language. The term is used most frequently of **linguistic minority** communities, since these are most likely to experience language shift. Many minority language communities attempt to secure language maintenance through various **language planning** activities, such as obtaining a role for the minority language in education.

language missionary A person who has a much greater role in influencing the course of linguistic change in a community than one would normally expect to be the case for a particular individual. Such individuals will usually be people who for some reason are respected and accepted as insiders by members of the community, but who differ from the other members of the community in their linguistic characteristics. The term was originally used by the Norwegian dialectologist Anders Steinsholt, but is now used by scholars working on the diffusion of linguistic changes in many parts of the world. Steinsholt described the strong linguistic influence exerted on a southern Norwegian rural community by small numbers of local men who had been away from the community on whaling expeditions and who later returned, bringing with them new non-local dialect forms they had acquired from other whalers.

language murder see **language death**

language planning Activities carried out by governmental, official or other influential bodies that are aimed at establishing which language varieties are used in a particular community, and subsequently at directing or influencing which language varieties are to be used for which purposes in that particular community, and what the linguistic characteristics of those varieties are to be. Language planning is normally undertaken in order to improve communications and education, and/or influence **nationism**, and/or achieve **language maintenance**. Language planning can be divided into two main types of activity, often labelled respectively **language determination** or **status planning**, and **language development** or **corpus planning**. (See also **language cultivation**.)

language shift The opposite of **language maintenance**. The process whereby a community (often a **linguistic minority**) gradually abandons its original language and, via a (sometimes lengthy) stage of **bilingualism**, shifts to another language. For example, between the seventeenth and twentieth centuries, Ireland shifted from being almost entirely Irish-speaking to being almost entirely English-speaking. Shift most often takes place gradually, and **domain** by domain, with the original language being retained longest in informal family-type contexts. The ultimate end-point of language shift is **language death**. The process of language shift may be accompanied by certain interesting linguistic developments such as **reduction** and **simplification**.

language use see **elaborated code**; **restricted code**

lect Another term for **variety** or 'kind of language' which is neutral with respect to whether the variety is a **sociolect** or a (geographical) **dialect**. The term is due to the American linguist Charles-James Bailey who, as part of his work in **variation theory**, has been particularly interested in the arrangement of lects in **implicational tables**, and the diffusion of linguistic changes from one linguistic environment to another and one lect to another. He has also been particularly concerned to define lects in terms of their linguistic characteristics rather than their geographical or social origins.

levelling One of the linguistic processes which may take place in a situation of **dialect mixture** and which can lead, together with **simplification**, to the development of a **koiné**. Levelling refers to the process whereby the number of variant pronunciations, words or grammatical forms that are present in the dialect mixture are reduced, as a result of focusing (see **focused**), to a smaller number of variants, usually one. Levelling usually takes the form of getting rid of forms which are used by only a minority of speakers or are in some other way unusual.

lingua franca A language which is used in communication between speakers who have no native language in common. For example, if English is used in communication between native speakers of Swedish and Dutch, then it is functioning as a lingua franca. Lingua francas which are used in a large-scale **institutionalized** way in different parts of the world include Swahili in East Africa, and French and English in West Africa. A **pidgin** language is a particular form of lingua franca.

linguistic area A geographical area, also known by the German term **Sprachbund**, in which long-term **language contact** has given rise to a large number of similarities between languages, even in cases where they are not historically closely related. The best-known linguistic area in Europe is the Balkans, where, amongst a number of other similarities, Albanian, Rumanian, Macedonian and Bulgarian all have definite articles that are placed after the noun, unlike languages in neighbouring areas or other languages with which they are more closely related.

linguistic insecurity A set of **language attitudes** in which speakers have negative feelings about their native variety, or certain aspects of it, and feel insecure about its value or '**correctness**'. This insecurity may lead them to attempt to **accommodate** to or acquire higher status speech forms, and may lead to **hypercorrection** on the part of individuals and **Labov-hypercorrection** on the part of social groups. Labov has suggested that it is normally the second highest status-group in a society that is most prone to linguistic insecurity.

linguistic market A translation of the French term *marché linguistique* due to Bourdieu and employed in Canadian sociolinguistic research by Sankoff and Laberge. They argue that it is possible to account for much sociolinguistic variability in language use in terms of the extent to which speakers' economic activity requires them to be able to use standard or other prestigious forms of language. They suggest that this may be a more important factor in determining linguistic behaviour than speakers' social class or social status background. Thus a working-class hotel receptionist may speak a **sociolect** not normally thought of as being typical of working-class speakers.

linguistic minority A social group within a nation-state or other organizational unit whose native **language** is different from the language which is spoken natively by the largest number of people in that state or unit. Thus Welsh speakers constitute a linguistic minority in Britain, Dutch speakers a linguistic minority in France, and Albanian speakers a linguistic minority in Greece. Some languages can be both majority languages (like German in Germany and Austria) and minority languages (like German in France and Rumania). Other languages may be minority languages everywhere they are spoken, such as Sami (Lappish) in Norway, Sweden, Finland and the Soviet Union.

linguistic relativity see **Sapir-Whorf hypothesis**

linguistic variable A linguistic unit, sometimes known as a **sociolinguistic variable**, initially developed by Labov in connection with his work in **secular linguistics** and **variation theory**, in order to be able to handle linguistic variation. Variables may be lexical and grammatical, but are most often phonological. A phonological variable may be more or less than a phoneme, but will be associated with a particular lexical set or group of words in which phonetic variation has been observed to occur, where that variation can be related to social variables or to other linguistic variables. A linguistic variable in many forms of British English is (h) – it is usual to symbolize linguistic variables by the use of parentheses – which stands for the presence or absence of /h/ in words such as *hammer*, *house*, and *hill*. Many speakers will sometimes pronounce /h/ in words of this type and sometimes not, whereas other speakers will always pronounce it – its presence is variable. The variable (h) does not refer to /h/ at the beginning of unstressed words such as *have*, *has*, *his*, *him*, *her*, since no speaker has an /h/ in these words unless they are stressed. The variable (h) is thus said to have two **variants**, /h/and ∅.

loan word see **borrowing**

location see **domain**

loss of face see **face**

macrosociolinguistics A term sometimes used to cover **secular linguistics**, the **sociology of language**, and other areas involving the study of relatively large groups of speakers. Compare **microsociolinguistics**.

marker In Labovian **secular linguistics**, a **linguistic variable** which shows **social stratification** *and* **style stratification**. In investigations of the **embedding problem** associated with linguistic change, markers represent an intermediate stage in the development of linguistic variables, having developed out of **indicators**, and having the potential to become **stereotypes**. Markers are typically involved in **change from below**.

matched-guise technique A technique used in work in the **social psychology of language** in order to investigate **language attitudes**. The technique involves playing recordings of different speakers reading aloud the same passage of prose but using different **accents**, **dialects** or **languages**. Subjects are asked to listen to the recordings and to evaluate the speakers, as best they can by listening to their voices, on parameters such as *friendly–unfriendly*, *intelligent–unintelligent*, *reliable–unreliable* and so on. The technique is called 'matched guise' because two of the speakers listened to by the subjects are, unbeknown to them, actually the same person, appearing in two different guises, i.e. using two different varieties of language. The assumption then is that, if subjects evaluate this speaker differently in his or her two different guises, the difference in the evaluation cannot be due to the speaker, or to his or her voice itself, but to reactions to his or her accent, dialect or language. Work by the British social psychologist Howard Giles has found that a person speaking in an **RP** accent is evaluated as being more intelligent but less friendly than that same person speaking in a local accent.

mesolect In a **social dialect continuum**, the **lect** or lects which have a social status intermediate between the **acrolect** and the **basilect**. In the Jamaican **post-creole continuum**, the mesolects are the varieties which are linguistically and socially ranged on the continuum between the **Standard English** acrolect and the Jamaican **creole** basilect.

microsociolinguistics A term sometimes used to cover the study of **face-to-face interaction**, **discourse analysis**, **conversation analysis**, and other areas of sociolinguistics involving the study of relatively small groups of speakers. Compare **macrosociolinguistics**.

modernization see **intellectualization**

monogenesis A term associated with the study of the world's **creole** languages and their history. Creole languages have many linguistic features in common. This is particularly true of the Atlantic creoles – those spoken on either side of the Atlantic Ocean, such as Krio in Sierra Leone, Sranan in Surinam, and Gullah in the United States. But it is also true, importantly, not only of very many creoles of English origin, but also of French-based creoles, such as Haitian Creole, and of Portuguese-based creoles. One explanation for these similarities is that the Atlantic creoles (at least) are monogenetic. That is, they are similar because they have a single common origin. They are all descended, this explanation claims, from the same **pidgin** language which was probably spoken in West Africa, where the original creole arose as a result of the slave trade, and from where it/they spread to many other parts of the world. Crucial to the monogenesis hypothesis is the **relexification** hypothesis, which explains how English, French and Portuguese creoles can all have the same origin. Like all theories of creole origins, this hypothesis is controversial.

monolingual see **monolingualism**

monolingualism The opposite of **bilingualism** and **multilingualism**. A sociolinguistic situation in which only one language is involved is said to be a **monolingual** situation. An individual who can speak only one language is said to be 'monolingual'.

multilingualism The opposite of **monolingualism**. A sociolinguistic situation in which more than one language is involved, usually involving also **language contact** and individual **bilingualism**. Note that many sociolinguists use the term 'bilingualism' to refer to individuals, even if they are trilingual, quadrilingual, etc., and reserve the term 'multilingualism' for nations or societies, even if only two languages are involved.

multiple negation A feature of the grammatical structure of most dialects of English which is, however, not found in **Standard English**. In sentences such as *I can't find none nowhere* and *I don't never do nothing*, more than one – or multiple – negative forms occur, whereas the equivalent sentences in the Standard English variety contain only one negative form each: *I can't find any anywhere* and *I don't ever do anything*. Multiple negation formerly occurred in all varieties of English, but has been lost from Standard English during the last three hundred years or so. Multiple negation is widely regarded as being 'incorrect', but this evaluation is simply due to the fact that it is a feature of lower status **sociolects**. It is a feature of the standard dialects of very many other languages, including French and Russian. Another name for multiple negation is **negative concord**, and it is also often called the **double negative.**

multiplex see **network strength**

Mundart see **traditional dialect**

mutual intelligibility The extent to which speakers of one variety are able to understand speakers of another variety. Mutual intelligibility may be a matter of degree – Swedish speakers can understand Norwegian more readily than they can Danish. Note too that the degree of intelligibility may not be entirely mutual – speakers of variety A may be able to understand speakers of variety B more easily than vice versa. And mutual intelligibility can also be acquired – speakers can learn to understand a variety that they initially had considerable difficulty with.

nationalism Feelings and sentiments that have to do with **nationality**. Nationalism is distinct from – and may in certain situations be in conflict with – practical issues concerning **nationism**. In a multilingual society such as India, nationism might suggest that a non-indigenous language such as English might be the best choice as the official language, while sentiments of nationalism might favour indigenous languages such as Hindi and Tamil.

nationality According to the American sociologist of language Joshua Fishman, a large-scale sociocultural group of people who feel themselves to be a social group distinct from other social groups. Nationality implies also that the group in question operates on a more than purely local scale. Nationality and **ethnic group** are not distinguished by all writers on **language planning** and **multilingualism**.

nationism A term used in discussions of **language planning** and **multilingualism**. According to Joshua Fishman, a nation is a political and territorial unit which is largely under the control of a particular **nationality**. Nationism then is a concept which has to do with the problems of administering such a political and territorial unit.

negation see **multiple negation**

negative concord see **multiple negation**

negative face see **negative politeness**; **positive politeness**

negative politeness A concept derived from the sociolinguistic work of Penelope Brown and Stephen Levinson on politeness. In this approach, politeness is concerned with the actions people take to maintain their **face** and that of the other people they are interacting with. **Positive face** has to do with presenting a good image of oneself and securing the approval of others. **Negative face** has to do with maintaining one's freedom of action and freedom of imposition by others. Negative politeness consists of acts which are designed to preserve or restore the hearer's negative face, by expressing the speaker's reluctance to impose his or her wants on the hearer, and/or by acknowledging the social distance between the speaker and the hearer. One way of doing this would be to say something like *I don't like to bother you, but . . .*

neighbour opposition see **hyperdialectism**

network strength A concept originally employed in linguistics by the British sociolinguists James Milroy and Lesley Milroy in their research in Belfast. The strength of a **social network** depends on the degree to which it is **dense** and **multiplex**. The density of a social network depends on the degree to which the people who form the social network all know each other. The multiplexity of a social network depends on the extent to which individuals are bound to one another by more than one relationship, e.g., two people might be cousins *and* friends *and* workmates.

non-prevocalic /r/ The consonant /r/ in English where it occurs before a consonant, as in *start*, or before a pause, as in *star*, rather than before a vowel, as in *starry*. 'Non-prevocalic' means 'not before a vowel'. Accents of English differ as to whether or not they have lost non-prevocalic /r/ through linguistic change over the past three hundred years or so. English accents which have retained the original pronunciation and have not lost non-prevocalic /r/ are known as **rhotic accents**.

non-rhotic accents see **rhotic accents**

nonstandard dialect In the case of languages which have undergone **standardization**, any **dialect** other than the standard dialect or standardized variety. Such dialects are normally heteronomous with respect to the standard variety. Nonstandard varieties of English may be referred to collectively by the label **nonstandard English**.

nonstandard English Any **dialect** of English other than **Standard English**. Nonstandard dialects of English differ from Standard English most importantly at the level of grammar. Examples of widespread nonstandard grammatical forms in English include **multiple negation**, past tense *done* rather than *did*, and the use of *ain't* rather than standard *isn't*, *aren't*, *haven't* and *hasn't*. One nonstandard dialect of English that has been extensively discussed in sociolinguistics is American **Black Vernacular English**.

NORM An acronym introduced by the Canadian linguist J. K. Chambers to describe the sort of informants typically sought after during their fieldwork by practitioners of **traditional dialectology**. Traditional dialectologists have often concentrated on 'non-mobile older rural male' speakers of the **dialect** under study because they have believed that such speakers were the most likely to speak the local traditional dialect in a 'pure' form, uninfluenced by the standard or by other dialects.

observer's paradox A term invented by the American linguist William Labov to describe the major methodological problem of **secular linguistics**. Secular linguistic research is based on analyses of linguistic data as this is obtained from people using a **vernacular variety** in a natural way in everyday speech situations in the **speech community**. However, observing and recording such speech is difficult because as soon as people realize that their language is the focus of attention, they will tend to speak in a less natural and vernacular manner. The observer's paradox is thus that 'what linguists want to do is to observe the way in which people speak when they are not being observed'. A number of different methodologies have been developed to attempt to overcome this paradox (see **participant observation** and **rapid and anonymous interviews**).

optional rules see **variable rule**

overgeneralization see **hyperadaptation**

panlectal grammar see **polylectal grammar**

participant see **domain**

participant observation An anthropological technique also used for carrying out sociolinguistic research. In sociolinguistics, work of this type is designed to overcome the **observer's paradox**. The methodology involves the fieldworker in becoming a member of the group under investigation, often over a considerable period of time, so that the group can be investigated from the inside. Research on the language used by the group can be carried out successfully because informal and long-term observation by an insider will not direct speakers' attention to their speech to an undue degree.

patois /ˈpatwa/ A non-technical term which has two rather different meanings. First, in many Caribbean communities, the local English or French-based **creole** language is referred to by its speakers as 'patois'. Secondly, **traditional dialects** of French are often referred to by French speakers as 'patois'. The term is also used by some French and English speakers to refer to any language which does not have a written form.

peer group A sociological term referring to a group of people that a person associates with and identifies with. Many of the peer groups studied by sociolinguists consist of teenage gangs or friendship groups, but any peer group to which speakers belong will be of importance for their linguistic behaviour, as discussed in sociolinguistic theories concerning **acts of identity** and **social networks**. **Lames** are speakers who are peripheral members of a particular peer group.

pidgin A variety of language without native speakers which arises in a **language contact** situation of **multilingualism**, and which operates as a **lingua franca**. Pidgins are languages which have been derived from a **source language** through **pidginization**. The degree of pidginization is such that **mutual intelligibility** with the source language is impossible or very difficult; and they have achieved a stable form through the processes of focusing (see **focused**) and **stabilization**. Many well-known pidgins are derived from European source languages such as English and Portuguese, but there are also many pidgin languages which are derived from non-European sources. (See also **jargon** (1) and **creole**.)

pidginization The processes of **admixture, reduction** and **simplification** which are associated with all imperfect adult second-language learning. Pidginization normally leads to the development of a **jargon** (1) or **pre-pidgin** only in multilingual situations in which access to the **source language** is minimal and where pidginization is therefore considerable. The jargon will develop into a pidgin only where there is a prolonged need for a **lingua franca** and where a stable social situation leads to focusing (see **focused**) and **stabilization**.

polite forms see **T and V pronouns**

politeness see **negative politeness; positive politeness**

polycentric standard A language in which **autonomy** is shared by two or more (usually very similar) **superposed varieties**. Examples include American, English, and Australian etc. **Standard English**; Brazilian and Portuguese Portuguese; and Serbian and Croatian Serbo-Croat. (See also **Ausbau language**.)

polylectal grammar A notion associated particularly with the work of the American linguist C.-J. Bailey, who argued that as speakers of a particular language are exposed, during their lifetimes, to more and more **dialects**, **varieties** or **lects** of that language, their increasing ability to comprehend these lects is due to their internalized knowledge or grammar of that language becoming extended to include many more lects than the one they actually speak. Linguists wanting to describe or account for this knowledge should therefore attempt to compose polylectal grammars which would reflect this competence in more than one lect. A polylectal grammar which incorporated all the varieties of a language would be a **panlectal grammar**.

positive face see **negative politeness; positive politeness**

positive politeness A concept derived from the sociolinguistic work of Penelope Brown and Stephen Levinson on politeness. In this approach, politeness is concerned with the actions people take to maintain their **face** and that of the other people they are interacting with. **Positive face** has to do with presenting a good image of oneself and securing the approval of others. **Negative face** has to do with maintaining one's freedom of action and freedom of imposition by others. Positive politeness consists of acts which are designed to preserve or restore the hearer's positive face, by stressing the speaker's empathy with and social closeness to the hearer. One linguistic way of doing this would be to link the speaker and hearer together by using the pronoun forms *we*, *us* and *our*.

post-creole continuum A social **dialect continuum** which results from **language contact** between a **creole** and its original **source language**, and consequent partial **decreolization** of the creole. **Acrolects** towards the 'top' of the continuum will have been decreolized in the direction of the source language much more than **basilects** towards the bottom, with intermediate mesolectal varieties having undergone intermediate degrees of decreolization.

post-pidgin A **language variety** which results from the partial **depidginization** of a **pidgin** language or **jargon** (1) caused by **language contact** between it and its original **source language**.

pragmatics A branch of linguistics which deals with the meaning of utterances as they occur in social contexts. Pragmatics is thus contrasted with **semantics**, which deals with purely linguistic meaning, and has connections with **discourse analysis**, **social context**, and the study of **speech acts**.

pre-pidgin see **jargon** (1)

purification The process associated with **decreolization** and **depidginization** in which the **admixture** which has taken place during **pidginization** is 'repaired' as a result of **language contact** between the **creole** or **pidgin** and the **source language**. Purification thus takes the form of the exclusion of forms originally from languages other than the source language and their replacement by source language forms.

quantitative sociolinguistics see **secular linguistics**

rapid and anonymous interviews One of the fieldwork techniques of **secular linguistics** designed to overcome some of the constraints of the **observer's paradox**. In this technique, the fieldworker conducts brief interviews in a public place with a large number of people in such a way as to obtain appropriate linguistic information from them without their realizing that their language is being investigated and without their being unduly inconvenienced. The most famous series of such interviews was the one conducted by William Labov in which he investigated the speech of shop assistants in department stores in New York by asking questions designed to produce the response 'on the fourth floor', thus obtaining from the informants potential instances of **non-prevocalic /r/**.

real-time studies Studies of linguistic change which attempt to investigate language changes as they happen, not in **apparent time** by comparing the speech of older speakers with that of younger speakers in a given community, but in actual time, by investigating the speech of a particular community and then returning a number of years later to investigate how speech in this community has changed. In secular linguistics, two different techniques have been used in real-time studies. In the first, the same informants are used in the follow-up study as in the first study. In the second, different informants, who were too young to be included in the first study or who were not then born, are investigated in the follow-up study.

reduction A part of the **pidginization** process which occurs in **language contact** situations where imperfect adult second-language learning takes place. Reduction – or **impoverishment** – refers to the process whereby large parts of the **source language** that are available to native speakers are lost or are not acquired by pidginizing non-native speakers. Comparisons between a **jargon** (1) or a **pidgin** and the source language will typically show that the source language has a larger vocabulary, and a larger repertoire of **styles**, phonological units, syntactic devices and grammatical categories. Reduction may be repaired by the process of **expansion** if **creolization** occurs.

register A technical term from sociolinguistics which is used to describe a language **variety** that is associated with a particular topic, subject or activity. In English, registers are characterized for the most part by vocabulary, but grammatical features may also be involved. Any activity may have a specific register associated with it, whether it is football, biochemistry or flower-arranging. Well-known technical registers include those of law and medicine: the medical register uses forms such as *patella*, corresponding to non-technical *kneecap*, and *clavicle*, corresponding to *collar-bone*. Registers can identify speakers as being members of a particular **peer group**, and are for that reason often labelled **jargon** (2) by outsiders who are not part of the group in question.

relexification A hypothesis used as part of the **monogenesis** theory of the origin of **creole** languages. This theory argues that all or some of them are very similar in their structures because some or all of them are descended from the same original West African **pidgin** form of Portuguese. In order to explain how Portuguese Pidgin could have given rise to English- and French-based creoles, it is necessary to invoke the hypothesis of relexification. This holds that when speakers of the original Portuguese Pidgin came into contact with, for example, native speakers of English, their language was relexified in the direction of English, i.e. the grammar and phonology of their language remained the same, but the Portuguese words were gradually replaced by words from English.

restricted code A concept developed by the British sociologist Basil Bernstein in connection with his work on language use, social class and socialization. Restricted code, originally called 'private language', is a form of language use which, according to Bernstein, is characterized by a high degree of inexplicitness and the taking of a fund of shared knowledge between speaker and hearer for granted. It is therefore not suitable for public use, Bernstein suggested, in situations where participants do not have much knowledge or many assumptions in common. Restricted code is thought of as lying at the opposite end of a continuum of types of language use from **elaborated code**. Bernstein argued that some working-class children in Britain were disadvantaged in the education system because they were able to use only restricted code. Restricted code has no connection with

nonstandard English or any other **dialect**. It is concerned, as part of a theory of **language use** and social structure, with the content of what speakers say.

rhotic accents Accents of English in which **non-prevocalic /r/** is pronounced, i.e. in which words like *star* have retained the original pronunciation /sta:r/ 'starr' rather than having the newer pronunciation /sta:/ 'stah', where the /r/ has been lost. Rhotic accents of English include nearly all accents of Scottish and Irish English, most accents of Canadian and American English, accents from the southwest and northwest of England, some varieties of Caribbean English, and a small number of New Zealand accents. **Non-rhotic** accents are those of Australia, South Africa, eastern and central England, some parts of the Caribbean, and a number of places on the eastern seaboard of the United States and Canada, as well as American **Black Vernacular English**.

roofing see **roofless dialects**

roofless dialects A term used mainly by German sociolinguists as a translation of German **dachlose** *Dialekte*. Roofless dialects are varieties which are not subject to **Überdachung** or **roofing**. They are dialects which are linguistically **heteronomous** with respect to some autonomous **standard variety**, but which are socially and politically outside that autonomous dialect's sphere of influence. An example of this is provided by the Alsatian dialects of German which are linguistically heteronomous with respect to Standard German, but whose speakers, because they live in France, do not have full educational or other access to Standard German. (See also **superposed variety**.)

RP Received Pronunciation. The regionless upper-class and upper-middle-class **accent** of British – mainly English – English which is associated with the BBC and is usually taught to foreigners learning 'British' English. The label 'received' is here used in an old-fashioned sense of 'being accepted in the best social circles'. The unusual regionless nature of the RP accent is probably the result of the unusual upper-class British educational system of non-regional residential private schools, known as the 'public schools'. Only a very small minority of the population of Britain – probably 3–5% – speak in this totally regionless way.

Sapir-Whorf hypothesis A hypothesis associated with the American scholars Edward Sapir and Benjamin Lee Whorf, also known as the linguistic relativity hypothesis. The hypothesis suggests that people's habitual thought patterns and ways of perceiving the world are conditioned to a certain extent by the categories and distinctions that are available to them in their native language. Speakers of different languages may therefore have rather different world-views, depending on how different the languages are from one another semantically and grammatically.

secular linguistics A view of sociolinguistics as a methodology – a way of doing linguistics – associated particularly with the American linguist William Labov, and sometimes also known as quantitative sociolinguistics or, less properly, **correlational sociolinguistics**. Secular linguistics has as its objective a series of goals which are no different from those of any other sort of linguistics, but works on the assumption that linguistic hypotheses and theories should be based on observations and analyses of **vernacular varieties** as these are used by ordinary speakers (e.g., not by linguists) in everyday **social contexts**. The research of linguists working in their offices on their intuitions concerning their own dialect of their own language needs to be supplemented and checked by work on (usually tape-recorded samples of) real language in real contexts. One of the particular concerns of secular linguistics is the attempt to achieve an understanding of linguistic change, and much work in this field is devoted to studying linguistic changes in progress.

semantics see **pragmatics**

sharp stratification In Labovian **secular linguistics, linguistic variables** are employed to investigate **social stratification** and **style stratification**. This stratification can take the form of **fine stratification** or 'sharp stratification'. In sharp stratification, the correlation between social or stylistic factors and linguistic variables reveals a relatively uncontinuum-like situation, with sharp breaks in linguistic behaviour, and thus in scores for linguistic variables, between one social group or style and another.

simplification A process involved in both **pidginization** and **koinéization**, and occurring also in other forms of linguistic change. Simplification refers most importantly to an increase in regularity in a language variety, e.g., the regularization of irregular verbs. It also refers to phenomena such as the loss of grammatical gender, the loss of case endings, and an increase in lexical transparency, e.g., the replacement of *optician* by *eye-doctor*.

slang Vocabulary which is associated with very informal or colloquial **styles**, such as English *batty* (mad) or *ace* (excellent). Some items of slang, like *ace*, may be only temporarily fashionable, and thus come to be associated with particular age-groups in a society. Other slang words and phrases may stay in the language for generations. Formerly slang vocabulary can acquire more formal stylistic status, such as modern French *tête* (head) from Latin *testa* (pot). Slang should not be confused with **non-standard dialect**. (See also **style**.)

social class dialect see **sociolect**

social context The totality of features in a social situation, involving location, participants, and their relationships with each other, which may influence speakers' linguistic behaviour, and which may, for example, lead to style shifting (see **style**). The 'study of language in its social context' is another way of referring to **secular linguistics**. The implication of this term is that it is important to study language as it is used by ordinary people in ordinary social situations, as well as or instead of the language of linguists, and language spoken in a laboratory. Secular linguistic research is thus based on the observing and recording of everyday speech rather than on the tapping of the linguist's intuitions about his or her own variety.

social dialect continuum see **dialect continuum**; **implicational scale**; **implicational table**

social dialectology see **dialectology; secular linguistics; urban dialectology**

social network An anthropological concept referring to the multiple web of relationships an individual contracts in a society with other people who he or she is bound to directly or indirectly to by ties of friendship, kinship, or other social relationships. This concept was introduced into sociolinguistic research by the British sociolinguists James Milroy and Lesley Milroy in connection with their research in Belfast. Lesley Milroy's book *Language and Social Networks* explains differential linguistic behaviour on the part of different social groups in terms of their different network structures and in particular in terms of **network strength**. (See also **peer group**.)

social psychology of language An area of the study of the relationship between language and society which examines **language attitudes** and looks at sociopsychological aspects of language use in **face-to-face interaction**, such as the extent to which speakers are able to manipulate situations by **code-switching**. An important tool in research in the social psychology of language is the **matched-guise technique**.

social stratification A term from sociology referring to a model of society in which a society is divided or ordered into horizontal 'layers' or 'strata', such as social classes or status groups, where people in the 'top' layers have more power, wealth, and status than those in the 'bottom' layers. In **secular linguistics**, **linguistic variables** are said to be subject to social stratification if they correlate in some way with this social hierarchy. Social stratification is contrasted in secular linguistics with **style stratification**. (See also **fine stratification** and **sharp stratification**.)

sociolect A **variety** or **lect** which is thought of as being related to its speakers' social background rather than geographical background. A **social class dialect** is thus a form of sociolect. (See also **acrolect**, **basilect** and **mesolect**.)

sociolinguistics A term used to describe all areas of the study of the relationship between language and society other than those, such as **ethnomethodology**, which are purely social scientific in their objectives. Sociolinguistic research is thus work which is intended to achieve a better understanding of the nature of human language by studying language in its **social context** and/or to achieve a better understanding of the nature of the relationship and interaction between language and society. Sociolinguistics includes **anthropological linguistics**, **dialectology**, **discourse analysis**, **ethnography of speaking**, **geolinguistics**, **language contact** studies, **secular linguistics**, the **social psychology of language**, and the **sociology of language**.

sociolinguistic variable see **linguistic variable**

sociology of language A branch of **sociolinguistics** which deals on a large or **macrosociolinguistic** scale with issues to do with the relationship between sociological factors and language, and in particular with issues to do with language choice. It thus incorporates the study of topics such as **multilingualism**, **language planning**, **language maintenance** and **language shift**.

source language In the study of **pidgin** and **creole** languages, the language from which a pidgin or creole is said to have derived, and which in particular has provided the bulk of its vocabulary. An English-based pidgin is thus a creole language which has resulted from large-scale **pidginization** of English by non-native speakers in a **language contact** situation, and the vocabulary of which is largely English in origin. The source language is often also known as the **target language**, but this is a less desirable term since it implies that the speakers responsible for the pidginization were actually attempting, unsuccessfully, to acquire the source language as such, which may well not have been the case.

speech act A term used in **discourse analysis**, **ethnography of speaking** and **pragmatics** for the minimal unit of analysis of conversational interaction. A number of speech acts combine to form a **speech event**. Speech acts, as defined by the American linguist and anthropologist Dell Hymes, include greetings, summonses, jokes, commands, apologies, and introductions.

speech community A community of speakers who share the same **verbal repertoire**, and who also share the same norms for linguistic behaviour, including both general norms for language use of the type studied in the **ethnography of speaking**, and more detailed norms for activities such as **style** shifting of the type studied by

secular linguistics. It is an important term in both the ethnography of speaking and in secular linguistics.

speech event A higher level unit for the analysis of conversational interaction than the **speech act**. A speech event consists of one or more speech acts. The term is used in **discourse analysis, ethnography of speaking** and **pragmatics**. Examples of speech events include conversations, lectures, and prayers.

spelling pronunciation A phenomenon due to a combination of literacy and **linguistic insecurity** in which the original pronunciation of a word is replaced by a newer pronunciation which more closely resembles the spelling. Twentieth-century spelling pronunciations which are now common in English include: *often* /ɒftən/, formerly /ɒfən/; *waistcoat* /weɪskoʊt/, formerly /wɛskɪt/; and *Ipswich* /ɪpswɪč/, formerly /ɪpsɪǰ/.

Sprachbund see **linguistic area**

stabilization A process whereby a formerly **diffuse** language variety that has been in a state of flux undergoes focusing (see **focused**) and takes on a more fixed and stable form that is shared by all its speakers. Pidginized **jargons** become **pidgins** through the process of stabilization. **Dialect mixtures** may become **koinés** as a result of stabilization. Stabilization is also a component of language **standardization**.

standard see **divergent dialect community**

Standard English The **dialect** of English which is normally used in writing, is spoken by educated native-speakers, and is taught to non-native speakers studying the language. There is no single **accent** associated with this dialect, but the lexicon and grammar of the dialect have been subject to **codification** in numerous dictionaries and grammars of the English language. Standard English is a **polycentric standard** variety, with English, Scottish, American, Australian and other standard varieties differing somewhat from one another. All other dialects can be referred to collectively as **nonstandard English**.

standardization The process by which a particular variety of a language is subject to **language determination**, **codification** and **stabilization**. These processes may be the result of deliberate **language planning** activities, as with the standardization of Indonesian, or not, as with the standardization of English.

standard languages see **koiné**

standard variety A variety of language which has undergone **standardization** and which has acquired **autonomy**.

status planning In **language planning**, status planning refers to decisions which have to be taken concerning the selection of particular languages or varieties of language for particular purposes in the society or nation in question. Decisions about which language or languages are to be the national or official languages of particular nation-states are among the more important of status planning issues. Status planning is often contrasted with **corpus planning** or **language development**. In the usage of most writers, status planning is not significantly different from **language determination**.

stereotype In **secular linguistics**, a **marker**, i.e. a **linguistic variable** which shows both **social stratification** *and* **style stratification**, which has attracted conscious attention and become the topic of overt comment. In investigations of the **embedding problem** associated with linguistic change, stereotypes represent a relatively late stage in the development of linguistic variables, having variants which have undergone extreme **stigmatization**, and, as a result, having become involved in linguistic **change from above**.

stigmatization Negative evaluation of linguistic forms. Work carried out in **secular linguistics** has shown that a linguistic change occurring in one of the lower **sociolects** in a **speech community** will often be negatively evaluated, because of its lack of association with higher status groups in the community, and the form resulting from the change will therefore come to be regarded as 'bad' or 'not correct'. Stigmatization may subsequently lead to **change from above**, and the development of the form into a **marker** and possibly, eventually, into a **stereotype**.

style In **sociolinguistics**, a **variety** of a **language** which is associated with **social context** and which differs from other styles in terms of their formality. Styles can thus be ranged on a continuum from very formal to highly informal or colloquial. In English, stylistic differentiation is most often signalled by lexical differences. Thus, in British English, *to slumber*, *to sleep* and *to kip* all mean the same thing, but are different stylistically. Styles are in principle distinct from **dialects** and from **registers**: nonstandard dialect speakers can and do employ formal styles, and standard speakers can and do use informal styles. Highly informal vocabulary is often referred to as **slang**. Changing from one style to another – or, better, moving along the continuum of styles – as the formality of a situation changes, or in order to change the formality of a situation, is known as **style shifting**.

style shifting see **style**

style stratification A term from **secular linguistics** which refers to the correlation of **linguistic variables** with **social context** and formality. A variable which is subject to style stratification in a speech community will show different use of different **variants** in different social situations. Thus, in many forms of British English, the [ʔ] variant of the variable (t) – the pronunciation of /t/ in words such as *bet* and *better* – occurs more frequently in informal than in formal styles. Variables which are subject to style stratification are known as **markers**.

superposed variety A **variety** which is 'placed above' a geographical dialect continuum in the sense that it has a social function of some kind over a wider geographical area than any of the continuum's constituent dialects. Most often, superposed varieties are **standard varieties** with the characteristic of **autonomy**. **Roofless dialects** are dialects above which there has been raised no autonomous superposed variety.

T and V pronouns A distinction made by many languages of the world between **familiar forms** of the second-person pronouns (corresponding to English *you*) and **polite** or **formal forms**. In sociolinguistics, these are known as T and V pronouns respectively, after the first letter of the familiar and polite forms in French, *tu* and *vous*. Most often, T forms are used as **address forms** for close friends and family members, while V forms are used to address strangers and other less intimate acquaintances, but there are also numerous differences between languages and dialects. In some languages, the V form was originally a second-person plural form, as in French. In others, as in the case of German *Sie*, it was originally a third person plural form.

taboo Behaviour which is believed to be supernaturally forbidden and/or highly immoral and/or very improper, and which is prohibited for irrational rather than rational reasons. Originally from a word found in the Polynesian languages with the form *tapu* or similar. Language taboo has to do with words and expressions which are supposed not to be used, and which are shocking, offensive, blasphemous or indecent when they are used. In **anthropological linguistics**, the study of linguistic taboo is of interest for what it tells us about the moral, religious and other values of a community. 'Swear words' are common examples of words which are subject to linguistic taboo.

talk see **ethnomethodology**

target language see **source language**

text linguistics see **discourse analysis**

topic see **domain**

traditional dialect An English term corresponding to German Mundart and French **patois** which refers to dialects which have been relatively unaffected by **koinéization** and/or by **dialect contact** with the **standard variety**. In the English-speaking world, traditional dialects are found only in England, northern Ireland, and the Lowlands of Scotland. They are linguistically conservative, compared to other dialects, and diverge linguistically from one another and the standard variety quite considerably. They are also associated particularly but not exclusively with the speech of **NORMS**. In England, pronunciations of a word such as *bone* as [bɪən], [ben] or [bwʊn] are typical of traditional dialects. Pronunciations typical of non-traditional or modern dialects include [boʊn], [bɔːn] and [bæʊn].

traditional dialectology The study of **traditional dialects** using the traditional methods of **dialectology**. The term can also be applied to research into urban and other non-traditional dialects involving the use of only older-style, i.e. non-**secular-linguistic**, methodology. The concepts of **isogloss**, **focal area**, and **transition zone** are due to work in traditional dialectology.

transfer see **admixture**

transition zone A concept from **traditional dialectology** and more recent work in **dialectometry**, **geolinguistics** (1), and spatial **dialectology**. Traditional dialectologists discovered early on in the history of the discipline that **isoglosses** for individual words and pronunciations rarely coincided with each other. One reaction to that finding was to suggest that there was no such thing as a dialect totally distinct from other dialects. This is, in most cases, strictly-speaking correct (see **dialect continuum**), but it is not simply the case that isoglosses are randomly distributed. Dialect features show different types of geographical patterning. Some geographical areas are crossed by no or relatively few isoglosses. These are **focal areas**. Focal areas are surrounded by transition zones which separate them from other focal areas. Transition zones are crossed by relatively large numbers of isoglosses, sometimes called **bundles of isoglosses**, few of them taking exactly the same course, but often running in roughly the same direction, depending on how far and in what direction innovations have spread outwards from the focal area. The transition from one 'dialect' (better: **dialect area**) to another thus appears to be gradual rather than abrupt.

turn-taking A term from **conversation analysis** used to describe the basic mechanism on which conversation is based. In a conversation, each speaker is entitled to 'turns', where a turn is his or her right and obligation to speak. Conversation is organized in such a way that only one speaker speaks at any one time, and changes of speaker occur. If speaker change does not occur, what results is a monologue, not a conversation. Turn-taking is thus an essential component of conversation.

Überdachung see **roofless dialects**

urban dialectology The study of **dialects** spoken in urban areas. This is sometimes contrasted with **traditional dialectology**, but urban dialects can also of course be studied using 'traditional' methods. Urban dialectology was also used as a term in the 1960s to refer to what is now called **secular linguistics**, but this usage is now inappropriate in view of the use of secular linguistic methods to study many other kinds of language **variety** than urban dialects.

Varbrul A computer program developed by the Montreal-based linguists Henrietta Cedergren and David Sankoff for the analysis of large amounts of data on **linguistic variables** obtained by **secular linguistic** research, and the development from this data of **variable rules**. This program greatly facilitates and speeds up the analysis of the differential effects of particular **constraints** on the selection of particular **variants** of a variable.

variable see **linguistic variable**

variable rule A concept introduced by the American linguist William Labov as a result of one of the major findings of secular linguistic research, namely that much variation in language is constrained by linguistic factors in a probabilistic kind of way which cannot adequately be represented as resulting from **optional rules**, since the rules are not truly 'optional' at all. Thus, the rule /t/ → [ʔ] /V—, which produces pronunciations such as *better* [bɛʔə] and *bet* [bɛʔ] in many forms of British

English, is not obligatory because pronunciations such as [bɛtə] and [bɛt] also occur. Neither, however, is it truly optional, since the frequency with which the rule operates is influenced by a number of **constraints**, such as whether the /t/ is or is not word-final, and whether or not the /t/ is followed by a vowel, which combine to influence the probability that the rule will apply.

variant see **linguistic variable**

variation theory Linguistic research which is based on empirical work in **secular linguistics** and which is concerned to apply the data obtained in such studies to the solution of problems of linguistic theory, such as how and why language changes, and what is the cognitive status of linguistic variability. Work on **polylectal grammars** and **variable rules** are examples of research in variation theory. The distinction between secular linguistics and variation theory is not a particularly clear or very important one.

variety A neutral term used to refer to any kind of language – a **dialect**, **accent**, **sociolect**, **style** or **register** – that a linguist happens to want to discuss as a separate entity for some particular purpose. Such a variety can be very general, such as 'American English', or very specific, such as 'the lower working class dialect of the Lower East Side of New York City'. (See also **lect**.)

verbal deprivation A now totally discredited notion developed by certain American educational psychologists in the 1970s, sometimes referred to as language deficit. They argued that certain (mostly Black) lower-class speakers of American English either (a) spoke dialects that were in themselves inadequate for the expression of abstract concepts and logical relationships, and/or (b) had not acquired enough of their native dialect to carry out such tasks, because of insufficient verbal stimulation. American linguists, led by William Labov, were able to show that the educational psychologists were arguing from a position based on (a) ignorance of the grammatical structure of English dialects, and (b) ignorance of **secular linguistic** methodology and of problems of research in this area, notably that concerning the **observer's paradox**. Some writers mistakenly identified verbal deprivation with Bernstein's **restricted code.**

verbal repertoire A term which refers to the totality of language varieties available to a **speech community**. Such repertoires will include different **styles**, and may also include different dialects in bidialectal or diglossic communities, and, in multilingual communities, different languages. Communities may reveal the range of their verbal repertoires through **code-switching**.

vernacular variety The indigenous **language** variety of a particular **speech community**. The term is used particularly to refer to dialects which are not national languages or **standard varieties** or **lingua francas**; to **nonstandard dialects** which have not been influenced by standard varieties; and to **styles** which are closely associated with informal contexts. In the **sociology of language**, vernacular languages are a focus of **language planning** debates about the extent to which education should be carried on through the medium of the mother tongue rather than the national language or languages. In **secular linguistics**, vernacular varieties are thought to be the most desirable object of study, being most regular and systematic because they have been least influenced by other varieties and by notions of **correctness**.

vitality A term used in the **sociology of language** for establishing a typology of language varieties. A **language** which has a community of native speakers is said to have the characteristic of vitality. **Varieties** which are undergoing **language shift** or **language death** have less vitality than other language varieties. **Classical languages** such as Latin and Sanskrit, which do not any longer have native speakers, and **pidgin** languages, which do not (yet) have native speakers, do not have the characteristic of vitality.